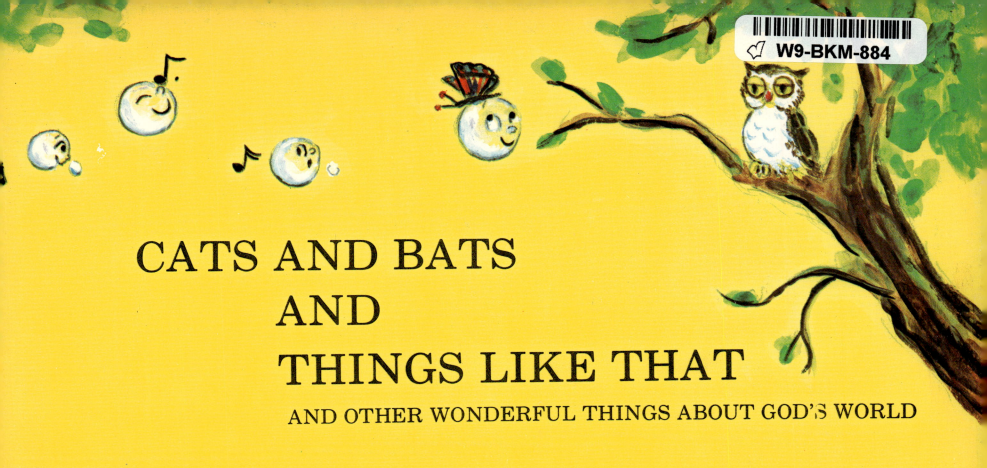

CATS AND BATS
AND
THINGS LIKE THAT

AND OTHER WONDERFUL THINGS ABOUT GOD'S WORLD

by V. Gilbert Beers

Illustrated by Juel Krisvoy

THE SOUTHWESTERN COMPANY

Nashville, Tennessee

©1973 by V. Gilbert Beers

CATS AND BATS
AND THINGS LIKE THAT

Cats and bats, and things like that
What are they doing?
Is it a parade? No, it is not.
Is it a picnic? Certainly not!
But all those cats and bats
and things like that
are doing the same thing.
Every one of them!
It is something you and I do.
But what are they doing?
They are just watching
to see where they are going.
But they are not all doing it
the same way.
Oh, no! Not at all!

Bats watch where they are going
when they fly somewhere.
Buy they do not do it with their eyes.
They send out sounds.
The sounds bounce back
from trees and things.
The bats hear the sounds.
They stay away
from the trees and things.

Men make big machines to do this, too.
They send out sounds that bounce back.
The sounds tell men where to find
things that they can't see.
Men call this sonar.
It costs thousands of dollars
to make a sonar machine.
But the bat gets his free.
God gives it to him.
His is a million times better
than our best sonar machine.
Men wish they could make sonar
as good as the bat's.
But they can't.
God does many things that we can't do.

God gave different work
to cats and bats.
So He gave them
different ways to see.
Bats send out sounds,
but cats see with their eyes.
So do lions and elephants.
And so do you!
It's part of God's special plan
for His very special world.
God made different kinds of eyes.
Some are big and some are little.
Some look like flying saucers.
God made some eyes
to see in the dark
and some to see His colors.
Since God made all the cats
and bats, and things like that,
He knew what kind of eyes
each one needed most.
But did you know that
God gave you
the best kind of eyes for you?
That's because He loves you
in a very special way.

GOD MADE SOME EYES
WITH DIFFERENT WINDOWS

Eyes have windows to let light in.
They are called pupils.
When it is dark, pupils get bigger
to let in more light.
When it is light, they get smaller.
God gave you round pupils.
He gave the horse
pupils that look like flying saucers.
They help the horse see
farther on each side.
Cats have pupils
that look like flying saucers, too.
But they go up and down.
That's because cats need to see
above and below
more than to each side.

GOD MADE SOME EYES
BIGGER THAN OTHERS

Owls have big eyes to see at night.
Their eyes are so big
that they cannot turn them.
Owls must turn their heads
instead of their eyes.
Owls need big eyes
to see their food at night.
But moles have tiny eyes.
They live in little tunnels
under the ground.
They do not need to see much.
They feel their way along.

GOD MADE SOME EYES
WITH DIFFERENT KINDS OF FILM

God gave two wonderful cameras
to each boy and girl and each animal.
Each eye is a moving-picture camera
with enough film to last a lifetime.
God gave you daytime eyes, so He put
color film in your cameras.
God gave cats nighttime eyes.
They can't see colors as well as you,
but they see much more at night.
The back of each eye is made
of little things called rods and cones.
Rods are like pencils.
Cones are like carrots.
Eyes with more rods see more at night.
Eyes with more cones see more color,
but do not see as well at night.

When God planned the world,
He did what was best for you.
How would you like
to sit in a tree at night,
looking for mice to catch?
If you were an owl,
you would like it very much.
You would have big eyes to see at night.
Would you trade places with your cat?
He doesn't care much
for flowers or sunsets.
But you do. You can see the colors.
And you know that God made them.

A mole is quite happy
with his tiny eyes.
But you wouldn't be.
You wouldn't want to live in a dark tunnel
and feel your way along.

God made your eyes
to see His wonderful world.
And to read His wonderful Word!
Don't forget to thank Him
for your good eyes.
And for giving the right kind of eyes
to cats and bats and things like that!

WHO PAINTS THE LEAVES?

Suddenly it is fall again.
Everywhere you look,
you see brightly colored leaves.
Red leaves.
Yellow leaves.
And leaves the color of oranges.

But only yesterday, it seems,
the leaves were all green.
Shiny green leaves.
Fuzzy green leaves.
And leaves as green as green gumdrops.

Where did all the colors come from?
Where did all the green go?
Who painted the leaves?
Was it Jack Frost,
as some books say?
No, it was not Jack Frost
who painted the leaves.
It was Someone Else
who did this wonderful work.
Someone very special.
His name is God.

God puts the colors
into the leaves.
He does it in His own wonderful way.
God does not use a big paint brush.
He does not use Jack Frost.
He does not even need the frost.
Then how does He do it?
How does God paint the leaves?

When summer comes,
and leaves grow,
God puts a certain something
into each one.
This certain something
is called chlorophyll.
It sounds like CLORO-FILL.
It paints the leaves green.
It helps the tree get its food
from water, air, and sunshine.
It helps the leaves turn
these things into sugar,
so the tree can have something to eat.
When it is fall,
something happens in each tiny stem
which holds its leaf to the tree.
It is time for the tree
to go to sleep for the winter.

The tree does not need new food
while it sleeps.
So God shuts off the stem,
just as you shut off
the kitchen faucet.
The water does not come
to the leaf now.
God also shuts off
the chlorophyll
and the green color.

When the green goes away,
you see another color
which was there all the time.
Some leaves had yellow in them.
It was there all summer.
But the green paint
of the chlorophyll
did not let you see the yellow.
Yellow leaves have
a special something in them.
It is called xanthophyll.
Do you like that word?
It sounds like ZAN-tho-fill.

Other leaves have
a special something, too.
It is called carotene.
That sounds like CARE-o-teen.
It makes the leaves
look red or orange in the fall.

Who paints the leaves
when fall comes around?
Who else, but God?
He takes care of each tiny leaf.
He feeds each tree
by His special plan.

He is the same wonderful God
who feeds you,
and takes care of you,
in summer, winter, spring, or fall.
So when you see the leaves,
think of Him,
and ask Him to help you be
all He wants you to be.

"To every thing there is a season . . .
He (God) hath made every thing
beautiful in His time . . . ."
Ecclesiastes 3: 1, 11.

WHAT WOULD YOU THINK?

What would you think,
yes, what would you think,
of a fish with an elephant's nose?
And how would a pig,
who just loves to dig,
like a beak where his funny snout grows?

A beaver's flat tail
wouldn't please a big whale,
or a horse, or an ugly rhinoceros.

And if a kangaroo
tried to trade his tail, too,
the zebra would raise such a fuss.

If a pelican's beak
sprang a leaky-type leak,
he might give it away to a moose.
But the moose might say "No,
it just shouldn't grow,
anywhere but the face of a goose!"

What would you think,
yes, what would you think,
if things weren't the way God planned them?

WHAT DO THEY DO WITH TAILS AND NOSES?

What do they do
with tails and noses?
Have you ever wondered why
God gave these things?
Have you thought how very different
all these things are?

When it gets dark outside,
and you go to bed to sleep,
you put your head on a soft pillow.
Mr. Fox does, too.
But his soft pillow is his tail.

If flies bother you this summer,
you will probably hit them
with a flyswatter.
God gave Mrs. Cow one, too.
Have you ever watched her
swishing the flies away with her tail?

You pick up peanuts and things
with your ten fingers.
Your fingers put your food
up to your mouth.
But Mr. Elephant has no fingers.
Even if he had some,
he would need to walk with them.
Mr. Elephant picks up his food
and puts it to his mouth, too.
But he uses his long nose.
Or do you call it a trunk?
That's the way God made him.

Do you like to sit on a chair?
It wouldn't be much fun
to stand up all day, would it?
God gave Mrs. Kangaroo
her own special chair.
Of course you know what it is!
It is her big, long tail.
She carries it everywhere.
When she wants to sit down,
she sits on her tail.

What would you do
without the telephone?
How would you talk.
with your friends after school?
Mr. Beaver has a telephone, too.
But he never pays a phone bill.
It's all free and it always works.
That's the way God planned it.

TREE School

What is Mr. Beaver's telephone?
That's right! His tail!
Whenever he wants to talk
with his beaver friends,
he hits his tail on the water.
His tail goes "slap"
instead of "ding-a-ling."
But it says the same thing.
"I'm calling to you."

When it's time to go fishing,
and you dig in the ground for worms,
What do you use to dig up the dirt?
Certainly not your nose!
But Mr. Pig does.
God put a special shovel
on Mr. Pig's nose,
so he can dig and dig,
and never have to sharpen it,
or buy a new one at the store.

How do you catch fish?
With a pole and worms?
Or a special net for the sea?
Nobody can catch fish
like Mr. Pelican.
While you fish with
your rod and reel
and net and things,
he dives through the air
or swims through the water
and catches more fish
than you can ever catch.

It's easy, if you have a nose
like Mr. Pelican's.
But you may call it a beak
if you wish.
But whatever you call it,
he catches fish.

What do they do
with tails and noses?
Have you ever wondered why
God gave these things?

You wouldn't want to swish a tail
to swat a fly,
or catch a fish with your nose,
or say hello with a slap on the water,
or pick up things like the elephant does.

No, of course you wouldn't,
for God made you to be YOU.
He made you so He could love you,
and so you could love Him, too.
Aren't you glad He did?

STRANGE LITTLE BOXES, FILLED WITH SURPRISES

Strange little boxes,
filled with surprises.
What do you think they are?
A hundred or more
in different colors,
boxes of red,
orange, and brown.
What are these boxes,
filled with surprises?
Boxes that look
so strange to see?

Some like porcupines,
or little black dots,
or shapes too strange
to tell what they are.
What do you think
of these strange little boxes?
What do you think they are?
Boxes that hide beautiful gifts,
sweet smelling flowers,
or many good things to eat.
What do you think
of these strange little boxes?
What do you think they are?

You wouldn't call them
boxes at all,
blowing through the sky
on a warm summer day,
or sticking to you
when you walk through the woods.
If you went to the store
to buy these strange boxes,
you'd find them all fixed
in pretty little packages,
lined up on racks
in the garden store.

No, you wouldn't call them
boxes at all,
as you ask the man for seeds.

Have you ever carved
a big jack-o-lantern,
making a face
on a big orange pumpkin,
digging out hundreds
of pumpkin seeds?
Pumpkin seeds
are strange little boxes
filled with green vines
and more orange pumpkins
for you to carve
into big jack-o-lanterns.

Surprises, surprises,
from strange little boxes.
Fluffy white popcorn,
or peanut butter,
or even a plate
of buttered green peas.
Coconut for candy,
or nuts for Christmas.
They're all surprises
from strange little boxes.
Strange little boxes
that you call seeds.

Strange little boxes,
with wings or tails,
or white parachutes
that sail in the wind.
Strange little boxes,
that float to new homes,
or fly on a summer breeze.
Strange little boxes
that hungry squirrels carry
and bury under the ground.
Strange little boxes
that hide in some burrs
and stick to your puppy or you.

Strange little boxes
that travel somewhere,
and show their surprises to you.
Strange little boxes,
filled with new life,
waiting to come out
when God says it is time.

What may come out
of strange little boxes?
What may come out for you?
Sunflowers and daisies
and cabbages, too.
Tall oaks and redwoods,
or marigolds bright.
Beans and radishes,
apples and gourds,
and watermelons sweet to eat.
What may come out
of strange little boxes?
What may come out for you?
Inside each seed
is something alive,
waiting to come out
when God says it is time.

Strange little seeds,
which look so dead,
when you bury them in the ground.
But then, one day,
new life appears,
vines or bushes,
plants or trees,
coming to help you,
for God says it is time.